This book belongs to:

____

Made in the USA
Coppell, TX
26 April 2022

77066472R00063